The Tone
of
Teaching

Max van Manen

Scholastic

Design by Kathryn Cole

Cover photo © SSC - Photo Centre Library - ASC

1st printing 1986   **Printed in Hong Kong**

Canadian Cataloguing in Publication Data

Van Manen, Max.
  The tone of teaching

(Bright idea)
ISBN 0-590-71631-X

1. Teaching.   2. Interaction analysis in education.   I. Title.

LB1033.V36 1986   371.1'02   C85-099836-0

For Mark and Michael

Contents

We need to be tactful

Danny is three hundred kilometers away from his home in a small northern mining town. The room of the clinic where they seat him on one side of the table is bright . . . and empty, except for a big box. The psychologist is a massive man, and when he enters he immediately sits down across from the boy. An assistant takes the mother and grandfather away to the other side of a one-way mirror. Danny is five years old. His development has seemed slow. Today he is about to undergo a series of diagnostic tests in this big city clinic.

The box on the table contains test materials. Danny doesn't know it, for the box is too high. Actually, he shows not the least bit of interest in the stuff the psychologist brings out of the box. The little boy looks very uncomfortable. He cries softly at first, and then begins to sob. It's clear he is not about to stop, so the psychologist returns the materials to the box. While the big man tells Danny there is no need for crying, he begins to write. At the same time he keeps an eye on the watch in front of him. Maybe Danny is inconsolable anyway, but the psychologist makes no attempt to comfort him. As he later explains, he does not want to interfere in Danny's reaction to the situation. He is merely making notes about the duration and intensity of Danny's crying.

A visiting psychologist is with the mother and grandfather on the other side of the looking glass. After almost ten minutes of tears, she can no longer bear Danny's distress. She enters the room and takes him on her lap. His sobbing stops and he calms down.

What is going on here?

It could have been done differently. The psychologist could have taken the five-year-old by the hand and said, "Let's go in here and see if there are some toys for us." They might have walked into the room and explored it together. If it had been a child-friendly space, they could have looked at pictures on the wall and got to know one another. As soon as they were comfortable with one another, they could have turned their attention to the box. The psychologist could have made invitational suggestions that they find out what might be in such an intriguing big box. Some toys, surely, for both of them. Maybe they could sit on the floor together and play.

Of course, it would have been even better (maybe even vital) if some of the observations had been made at the child's home where the psychologist could "test" not only the child but also the living space, the family sphere, the everyday lifeworld of the child. Many tests can easily be done in natural settings with the child's own familiar objects and toys. Then subsequent so-called "diagnostic" tests merely become interpretive means of finding out how to help the child have positive experiences in growing up.

What went on in that large, central clinic in that big city? That psychologist was steeped in child development literature, was well able to handle diagnostic instruments, wrote precise scientific reports: a thorough clinician. He had diagnosed hundreds of children. Yet the big man seemed quite insensitive to the way Danny experienced the situation: the strange room, the big man with the box, mom and grandpa leaving him all alone. The essential first question was not asked: "How is the child experiencing this situation?" That professional had a good deal of clinical "knowledge" but lacked "thoughtfulness." Thoughtfulness is a special kind of knowledge.

———————

At the end of a school day a janitor sees two boys stuffing pieces of wood in the outside door lock, perhaps so they can get into the school at night. The next morning the principal confronts one of the boys, who refuses to give his friend's name. The angry principal tells the boy that vandalism is a crime and that no child should get away with damaging public property and putting extra burdens on taxpayers. The boy is uncooperative and is suspended from school for five days.

What else does one do with a thirteen-year-old boy who refuses to be a fink? Let him off the hook? That seems unwise. But trying to show the value of private property and public good to a boy who is devoted to another principle altogether seems unproductive.

There is a prior pedagogic question to be answered: "What is the situation the child finds himself in?" Or, even more: "How does the child experience the situation?" No matter how well-meaning many of us are as pedagogues, our words and actions may address themselves to a situation the child is not part of. A school administrator is not a manager, a policeman, a judge. He is first of all an educator. And so this principal should wonder, "What is to become of this boy? How does this event fit into his life? What meaning does it have for him? What should I say, how should I act to make sure he can learn from this experience? How can I allow this young person room for the youthful living that is appropriate for his age? How can I nurture him so he will grow up to be a responsible adult?"

Imagine the principal at work behind his desk. There is always something officious and solemn about that. A boy is sent in, stands and waits, and the principal looks up briefly and says with the tone of a principal, "You are the one who tampered with the school door lock?" The boy, somewhat defiantly perhaps, nods — or expresses frozen uncommunication. The principal returns to his work and the boy stands there. Time goes by. There are several minutes to reflect. What is it like to stand waiting like that? Would it be a positive or a negative experience for the boy? That depends in part on the kind of person the principal is. Is he the God of the school? What is it like to stand waiting in front of a God?

Or would it be better for the principal to say, "Look, I know you don't want to tell on your friend. But I can't let you off like that. After all, this is our school and . . ." It would depend on what "our school" meant for the boy, and why he wanted to break into it in the first place. A tactful principal knows what to say and what not to say, what to mention and what to pass over or leave unsaid. The ability of a principal to enter into the world of a child is thoughtfulness.

———————

"I really would like to hear you practice the violin," says mother. A sour situation. What is supposed to be a satisfying experience, fun even, for parent and child, becomes pure obligation. Already mother's voice bears a tone of anticipated disappointment. Every day another battle. And the parent hears herself think, "Why can this child not show some enthusiasm, some gratitude for all my sacrifice?"

But the child hears something else. Mother wishes she would play the violin with enthusiasm. But also, quite clearly, mother does not really enjoy the violin practice. It's a chore for her too. That's evident from the businesslike manner in which the daily practice is set in time and space. Violin practice is a contractual encounter between this mother and this child, and both wish it were over before it even starts. Both approach the practice with apprehensive tenseness. Soon the child says, "I'm tired, Mama. Can I do it later?" The violin is held with resignation and nothing is uglier than an unwilling body holding an awkward musical instrument.

10

Children are sensitive to subtle signs of mood, of atmosphere. Undeniably, making music together is not really being enjoyed in this family. Mother says angrily, "All right, that's it. I'm sick and tired of your attitude. Maybe we should sell your violin, or give it to some child who knows how to appreciate music."

Elsewhere in the same neighborhood a father lifts a cello out of its case. He lovingly tunes it. There is a certain patience and discipline in his gestures. No rushing. This is a special moment, a kind of interlude, a time to be enjoyed for its own sake. The cello sings a languid song. This is not a call to duty but an infectious invitation. There is something compelling in the way the house fills up with sound. The body is responsive, follows the music. Michael walks into the room and looks, listens, smiles. Then, as surely as the cello sings, he opens his violin case and sets the instrument to his chin and shoulder. The tones harmonize. It is remarkable how the five-year-old can find the right entrance to his father's melody. The father smiles, surprised. Good. But in a way he expected this; he had carefully selected the right chords. Soon certain tonal phrases are exchanged, picked up, repeated. The ear tastes them for their roundness, fullness, and blend. "Now try it like this. Yes, on the E string."

Making music together is hard to distinguish from practice and exercise in this situation. A routine quality may well be worked into such a practice, but the exercise now is experienced as a healthy workout. It elevates the spirit. Routine is not only a voluntary, familiar path, it can offer something new: harmony and melody feeding both body and mind.

___

What do these examples show us about the pedagogy of bringing up children? Simply this: pedagogy is both a complex and a subtle affair. Specific rules, or even general principles, are difficult to formulate. Some adults seem to strike just the right tone with children. Others constantly flounder in their dealings with them. The difference is not necessarily that some adults have read more about parenting or teaching than others. Reading educational literature can give us important knowledge, but that knowledge is external. It does not necessarily make us more thoughtful or more tactful in our day-to-day relations with young people.

Thoughtfulness, tactfulness, is a peculiar quality that has as much to do with what we are as with what we do. It is a knowledge that issues from the heart as well as from the head. We can imagine the mother in our example complaining to the father who plays the cello. The father says to her, "Why don't you sing along or play along?" Now imagine the mother taking this advice to heart. Will it work? All we can say is that it may. We can never predict success. No two children are alike or experience a situation in exactly the same manner. What is even more important, will the mother be able to generate the same invitational atmosphere as the father does? This is a very fragile and subtle thing. And unfortunately (or fortunately) there are no rules that will ensure the right kind of thoughtfulness and tact.

Pedagogic thoughtfulness is sustained by a certain kind of seeing, of listening, of responding. Out of this basis of thoughtfulness, tact in our relationship with children may grow.

Children teach possibility

The child who loves wakes not only to the
morning but also to his father and mother who
sleep too much and often are asleep throughout
their lives. We all have a tendency to sleep
through things, yet, with the coming of a child,
there is a new being who awakens us and keeps
us awake with means that are not ours, a being
who operates in a way different from our way
and who appears every morning as if to say,
"Look, there is another life; you can live better
than you do."

Maria Montessori, *The child in the family*. New York: Avon
Books, 1970.

Children are not there primarily for us. We are
there primarily for them. Yet they come to us
bearing a gift: the gift of experiencing the possible.
Children are children because they are in the
process of becoming. They experience life as
possibility. Parents and teachers are good
pedagogues when they model possible ways of
being for the child. They can do that if they realize
that adulthood itself is never a finished project. Life
forever questions us about the way it is to be lived.
"Is this what I should be doing with my life? Is this
how I should spend my time?" No one can
reawaken these questions in us more powerfully
and more disturbingly than a child. All that is
required is that we listen to children and learn from
them. In this, children are our teachers.

We pedagogues (teachers and parents)
willingly open ourselves to children. This means
that we do our utmost to understand what it is like
to be in the world as a child. More concretely, I do
my very best to understand the situation of *this*
child. How does *this* child experience life in its
multifaceted dimensions?

Placing myself beside my student as a teacher
(my child as a parent) is very personal and can be

very fragile. Take the case of Hans and his grandparents. Hans is four, and his grandparents live a long way away. Naturally they want to make the most of any visit. So when they go to see another relative they take Hans along in their big shiny car. Hans is excited. There are many buttons on the dashboard. There are many new places to be traveled through. "What is that building, Grandma? Look at that dog! What's this button for, Grandpa?"

But his questions fall mostly on deaf ears. The grandparents are having their own conversation and they only occasionally throw a comment or question in Hans's direction, like candies to keep him occupied and pacified. Hans's words are not even heard. They like to have him along, but they do not invite him to be present in a personal sense. When Hans comes home he is unusually quiet, and only after mother's prodding does he remark, "I had nobody to play with."

As an adult, I embody possible ways of being for the child. I see the child trying on my gestures, my ways of seeing and doing things, my ways of reacting, my ways of spending time. And as I see that happening, I am confronted with my own doubts. Is this the way I *want* my child to act and be? And if not, is it the way I want myself to act and be? The child becomes my teacher. As he or she tries out possibilities, I am reminded of the possibilities still open to myself. In this experience of pedagogic possibility lies the truth of the saying that children make us feel young again. Children in their trying out express that there is hope, that there is possibility of living life differently, and better. And once again I grasp that hope for my own life.

For some, bringing up children becomes a self-serving, narcissistic enterprise. There are parents (and teachers) who are physically present but absent in spirit, given over to selfish wants and

needs. There are also parents and teachers whose
lives seem lived in competition or conflict with the
lives and interests of their children. It is sad that
adults can neglect children, turn deaf ears to them,
be appalled or horrified by them, vilify and abuse
them, disown and abandon them. Their worst
punishment may well be a constant feeling of
remorse, a lasting regret that their personal
preoccupations robbed them of opportunities to
experience close relationships with their children.
Those children will probably need the rest of their
lives to make sense out of the disarray of their
childhood memories.

But true teachers (parents) experience the
personal hope that is derived entirely from
child-ness. There is a paradox here. I experience
this child's life as more important than my own,
and the result is that I must now take a closer look
at my own. I must question and reshape it. Before I
had this child I could abuse myself, if I wished,
with bad habits. I could live life quite unaware of
the deep needs of others. But because I live with
and love this child, I can no longer live comfortably
with my old self. The education of the child turns
into self-education.

There are educators who believe that their own
education is complete. They will probably try to
impose a taken-for-granted set of beliefs and
values. Inevitably such "education" turns into a
pedagogy of oppression — an authoritarian form of
domination of adults over children. The
"completed" educator tends to see children as
incomplete. No need then to listen to children.
Impossible to learn from them.

Pedagogy is child-watching

How does a parent or teacher *see* children? Is there a unique pedagogical way of seeing children, different from the way other people would see them? A strange question perhaps. Given that seeing is a sensory act, don't we all see children the same way? For example, we see the same figure, the same movement, the same child skipping rope or painting a picture.

But we never see anything purely. How and what we *see* depends on who and how we are in the world. How and what we see in a child is dependent on our relationship to that child.

I see a child skipping rope in the street, and I pause and smile. I see a youthful bounce, the commanding rhythm of a rope — and perhaps a memory. I recognize this rhyme. Times do not change. When the child stops, I still feel the snap against my feet. Regret fills me. I wish I could revisit the old school playground. But then I come to myself. My childhood place is thousands of kilometers away. It is not likely I would see it again as I knew it. I turn away from that child and resume my walk. I saw a child, a rope, a game. Sight and sound collaborated to make me feel the rope against my feet. Then I saw regret, nostalgia. Then I went on my way.

The teacher sees Diane skipping rope. He sees much more than a passerby can see, for he has known her for more than a year. She skips away from the other children, and he wonders what it will take for Diane to become one of them. She is academically the best achiever of her class, but her achievements are not the product of some irrepressible raw intelligence. Diane earns her accomplishments with a grim fervor that saddens the teacher. She has an over-achieving mother who fosters ambitious goals. Diane's mother intends to have herself a gifted daughter. Diane complies. She earns her mother's favor, but at the price of childhood happiness, her teacher thinks. As he sees her skipping, he observes her tenseness and contrasts it with the relaxed skipping of the others. It is the same tenseness that betrays her anxiety with every assignment, every test. Diane marches rather than skips through the hoop of the rope.

The teacher also sees how Diane's eyes are turned to a half dozen girls who skip together with a big skipping rope. One of the girls returns her glance and gestures for Diane to come. Diane abruptly stops. The rope hits her feet and she turns toward the school door.

What does the teacher see? A lonely girl who can relate to classmates only by constantly measuring herself by competitive standards. If only she could develop some personal space, some room to grow and develop social interests just for herself, away from her mother. The teacher is hopeful, for in Diane's eyes he has spotted desire — a desire to be accepted by her classmates. Who knows, some "thoughtfulness," some pedagogical tact may just nudge Diane closer to the shared social space of her possible friends.

We are contrasting the way a passerby sees a skipping girl with the way a teacher sees Diane. The teacher has a pedagogic interest in the life of the child. He stands in pedagogical relationship to her, and he cannot help but see the child as a whole human being involved in self-formative growth.

There is an acute danger in thinking professionally about children. Child psychologists, instructional consultants, curriculum developers, resource personnel, principals, school counselors, evaluation specialists, learned professors, we are all in danger of thinking and talking about children in abstract ways, in categories. The theoretical

17

language of child "science" so easily makes us look past each child's uniqueness toward common characteristics that allow us to group, sort, sift, measure, manage, and respond to children in preconceived ways.

Once I call a child "a behavior problem" or a "low achiever," or once I refer to him or her as someone who has a specific learning style, a particular mode of cognitive functioning, then I am inclined immediately to reach into my portfolio of instructional tricks for a specific instructional intervention. What happens then is that I forego the possibility of truly listening to and seeing the specific child. Instead, I put the child away in categorical language, as constraining as a real prison. Putting children away by means of technical or instrumental language is really a kind of spiritual abandonment.

A teacher is a child-watcher. That does not mean a teacher can see a child "purely" without being influenced by the philosophic view that teacher holds of what it means to be human. One cannot adequately observe children without reflecting on the way one looks at them. All I am saying here is that a teacher must observe a child not as a passerby might, or a policeman, or a friend. A teacher must observe a child pedagogically. That means being a child-watcher who keeps in view the total existence of the developing child.

Diane conducts herself in a certain way on the playground, and the teacher watches quietly and wishes she could bring her academic effort and her personal life into better harmony. The teacher thinks of specific ways influence might be brought to bear on Diane.

The teacher has an understanding of the child's development that is simultaneously engaged and reserved, close and distant. On the one hand, he or she must watch the child with concern, and herein lies both engagement and maximum subjectivity. And on the other hand, the teacher must watch the child's total field of limits and possibilities, and herein lies the need for reserve and distancing.

Teachers are oriented to children in a special way. In some ways not unlike parents, but still not *quite* like parents. Like a parent, the teacher is concerned with the child's maturation, growth and learning. But the teacher has a special interest in certain aspects of a child's growth, while realizing that the total development must be kept in view. By exemplifying a certain standard or norm, educators mobilize their influence to help children gain insight into their own interests. Thus, a math teacher shows how mathematics requires an orientation to order and analytic idea.

In some sense, the most personal relationship between adult and child is the parenting relationship. Only a father and mother can watch a child with truly fatherly and motherly eyes. But a teacher too enters a very personal relationship with a child. At the same time, there is a distancing which makes the teacher a special pedagogic observer. By knowing *this* child, a teacher can hold back superficial judgment about him or her. The word "observing" has etymological connections to "preserving, saving, regarding, protecting." The teacher serves the child by observing from very close proximity while still maintaining distance.

Every child needs to be seen

Michael:

Michael rushes to the door of his kindergarten. For him school is the greatest place to be. His father is a few steps behind and sees Michael straining to open the heavy door. The teacher is at her desk talking to a parent as the little boy walks into the classroom. Michael is quickly at her side, his eyes beaming. He's brought something to show and share. "Look, teacher. Look who's here." But the teacher is too busy, oblivious of Michael and the other children now entering the room. Michael's father is uneasy. He has noticed such incidents before. Yesterday Michael was pulling at the teacher's clothes to say goodbye, but she was busy talking to a parent then too and ignored him. Most of the other children walk straight past the teacher to take off their coats and hang them in their assigned places. Some others, like Michael, linger around her, without any response. By now Michael has given up trying to get her attention and is busy taking off his coat. "Well, goodbye, Michael," says his father, giving him a wink. "See you later. Have a good morning."

Mark:

Mark is in a different kindergarten. He too is followed into school by his father, who knows the boy's shyness. But the classroom door is wide open and the teacher stands in the doorway. She greets him with a warm handshake and a gentle nod. "Good morning, Mark." She notices that he is holding a book for show and tell, and she is immediately interested. Mark beams with pleasure and anticipation.

Mark's father notices that a parent stands behind the teacher, obviously waiting to discuss something. But first the teacher is totally absorbed in her usual practice of seeing each child who enters the classroom. She does the same at the completion of each school day. Every child receives a handshake and an appropriate comment that in some special way gives meaning to the end of the school day.

A significant difference? I think so. An accidental difference? Not likely. It would be too harsh to say that Michael's teacher has no eye for the children entrusted to her class. But not only does Mark's teacher see her children, the children thoroughly experience being seen. Being seen is more than being acknowledged. For a child it means *experiencing* being seen by the *teacher*. It means being confirmed as existing, as being a person and a learner. Not all seeing has this quality, of course. Lucky is the child who is being seen regularly with pedagogic discernment.

A real teacher *knows* how to see children — notices a shyness, a certain mood, a feeling of expectation. Real seeing in this sense uses more than eyes. When I see a child for whom I have responsibility, I see the child with my body. In the sensory quality of my gesture, the tilt of my head, a certain bounce in my feet, my body *sees* the child's manner of starting this day, and the child experiences being seen. So to really *see* a child at the beginning and completion of each day is to give that child his or her place in specific time and space.

Such a teacher knows that each school day has a specific wholeness, a color, a significance for each child. No school day can be repeated. It may seem a cumbersome ritual to shake each child's hand twice each day, but the teacher who makes the effort *touches* each child. How easy it is, otherwise, to let days go by without being in touch with certain children. The quiet and "easy" child can remain untouched for quite some time.

Similarly, the disturbing behavior of the difficult or "problem" child is often related to the child's need to receive attention. Especially in our large comprehensive high schools, there are many young people who move from class to class, from school year to school year, without ever really being seen by teachers. These are the children no teacher really knows, about whom teachers cannot speak. Some teachers in large institutions are responsible for hundreds of youngsters each day. Such contexts breed technocratic acts. Even those teachers who try to interest and inspire students rarely have an opportunity to discover how interest is experienced and lived by their students. Such a teacher is a minister without congregation. Few teachers make real "home" visits with their students.

Naturally, greeting and saying goodbye must be more than mere ritual. The value of this practice is that it sets the tone for interpersonal relations and situations. Shaking hands permits a teacher to both *feel* the child's way of being and simultaneously give it form and content. The good teacher recognizes a shy handshake, a timid one, a hand full of energy, an absent-minded child, a confident one. A good teacher knows how to respond tactfully to a hand: what to mention, what to pass over, what to notice.

The moment of the handshake is the moment of the teacher being there for the child, and the child for the teacher. In each true handshake there is a moment of mutuality which shuts out the rest of the world. In it lies the possibility of true interpersonal contact. As our hands respond to the gesture of each other's approach, we create shared space. Our eyes meet, and for an instant we are there only for each other. Similarly, the saying goodbye at the end of the day communicates what the day has meant. It provides oppportunity for a brief monitoring and reflecting on the day just past.

The teacher can bring forward a meaningful moment of the day in a reflective statement such as, "You were very helpful to Hans today, Maria." Or, "We all enjoyed the fine story you told us, Jenny." Or, "I was amazed at the amount of work you accomplished, Robert." Or, "Goodbye, David, don't forget to show us the seashells you wrote about."

Children also teach us hope and openness

This is what Helen says:

> Adults let us feel there is no hope for us. Even
> my parents seem to think the kind of life they
> had is now beyond the reach of young people.
> To feel there is no hope . . . I think this is the
> most difficult thing. Myself, I seem to have
> highs and lows. I'm depressed when I think
> about the chances of a nuclear catastrophe.
> There are times when I feel like many of my
> friends: that none of us will reach the age of
> thirty. But — you know — you can't think of
> nuclear war all the time. I think of it often, but
> on the whole I am pretty hopeful. I want to have
> a good life, a family, kids perhaps. The difficult
> thing is that it is hard to have hope at times
> when even your parents don't encourage you to
> feel hopeful.

This is Tim:

> Sometimes I feel really depressed, like there's
> no point in going to school because I'm going to
> die soon in a nuclear bomb explosion. And I feel
> really resentful toward the older generation
> who left us this mess. Their lives may be just
> about over but ours have only just begun . . . I
> want to live. I want a chance to experience good
> things while I'm young. And I feel bad that I
> have to worry about pollution and nuclear war.
> It's an awful responsibility young people have
> to bear. The older generation is just dumping all
> these things on us, and what can we do?

Terry:

> It seems that I am living both in the best and the
> worst of times. Generally I like my life. I have
> lots of fun with my friends and life is quite
> exciting. But I'm also often quite scared . . . I
> wonder what is to become of me. I'm in the last
> year of school and I haven't the faintest idea of
> what to do with myself once school is over for

me. Will I find a job? I am afraid of the future. I
would like to feel secure — that I will be able to
afford a place of my own . . . have a family. But
there may not be any jobs for me to get. And
college is out of the question. So what can I do?
I'm quite worried about these things and I talk
about it with my friends. Many of them feel the
same way.

This is Jessica:

Hardly a day goes by that I don't think of the
possibility of a nuclear disaster. But I don't
really know what I could possibly do. When
there is a peace march, I usually participate. But
it seems that no one is ever listening. Politicians
don't seem to care, so it seems I have to learn to
live with it . . . knowing that one day suddenly
everything may come to a terrible end. It could
be tomorrow. It is in my dreams . . . my
parents, my brother, we all die. It's so absurd,
and I don't know what to do with it.

What do we say to these children? That's the
way they experience our age. It is hard to listen to
them and not see and hear our own failings. They
tell us we have burdened them with a living fear of
ultimate horror and wasted life. Worse yet, they
voice the accusation that we have heaped on them
the responsibility of transforming this madness into
something that will make sense in a child's life.

The question must be posed whether we have
the right to ask children to assume a responsibility
which is not theirs, but ours. We are the
pedagogues called on to demonstrate and model
active hope for our children and for our world. But
it is difficult not to smile cynically at any positive
program in the shadow of "The Bomb." It seems
easier to shrug fatalistically, to despair, to sigh that
the worst is yet to come. Yet those of us who live
with children cannot afford to be so nihilistic; we
cannot abandon the pedagogic place we occupy in
the lives of our children. Children are hope.

We hear that in Sweden women may refuse to have any more babies as long as disarmament policies remain ineffective. A hopeless world has no room for children. But for as long as there are children in your life, in your home, in your classroom, have a look, a good look, a "universe" look. What you see is hope. Having seen your children, hope is now present in your life. In living with children, new parents often gain the sudden conviction that the world should — *must* — continue to exist. Now that I am father to this child I can no longer turn away from the political insanities that threaten the world. I experience my children as living hope. I must act. Hope has activated me.

Hope is there from the very beginning, from the first stirring of the fetus. However mixed up and confused the feelings of expectant mothers and fathers may appear, one of the earliest and deepest sensations is the experience of hope, which particularizes itself in thoughts such as, "I hope this baby will be healthy." The woman who is expecting a child is literally inhabited by hope.

I offer you a new definition of pedagogue. Those who are inhabited by hope are true fathers, true mothers, true teachers to children. Pedagogic hope animates the way a parent or teacher lives with a child, and it gives meaning to the way an adult stands in the world, represents the world to the child, takes responsibility for the world, and embodies or stylizes the forms of knowledge through which the world is known and explained to children. If we know how to listen to children, we know what punishment will befall us when we fail or refuse to show how a life of hope is to be lived. Our irresponsible example may turn entire generations of young people into cynics, adults without hope, grown-ups who have no sense of commitment, who refuse to model how life is to be lived. The German author Günter Grass knew this well. In *The Tin Drum* Oskar simply refused to grow up, for he had no reason to do so.

Hope is not just a passive kind of optimism that somehow things will work out in the end. Hope implies life commitment and work. Even in the most absurd and painful of circumstances we cannot and must not give up on our children. How ironic! So much can go wrong in our lives, especially these days, and yet it is precisely in this time of hopelessness that the vulnerability of our children makes hope once again a possible human experience.

To be a parent or a teacher is to have expectations and hope for a child. But "hope" is only a word, and words have ways of becoming overworked, clichéd, superficial, empty sounds. So we must examine how living with children is experienced as hope, how what we do is hope. The most important aspect of our living hope is a way of being with children. It is not what we say and do, first of all, but a way of being present to the child. We may say, "I hope that . . . " with reference to particular expectations and desires: "I hope that my child will do well in school," or, "I hope he can do his homework," or, "I hope she'll get along." These are the hopes which come and go with the passing of time. But children make it possible for adults to transcend themselves and say, "I hope. I live with hope. I live life in such a way that I experience children as hope."

This experience of hope distinguishes a pedagogic life from a non-pedagogic one. It also makes clear that we can only hope for children we truly love, in a pedagogic sense. What hope gives us is this simple confirmation: "I will not give up on you. I know you can make a life for yourself." Hope refers to all that gives us patience, tolerance and belief in the possibilities for our children. Hope is our experience of the child's possibilities. It is our experience of confidence that a child will show us how life is to be lived, no matter how many disappointments we may have experienced. Thus hope gives us pedagogy. Or is it pedagogy that gives us hope?

Let us focus for a moment on modern "behavioral objectives" or "management by objectives" talk. The industrial model has deeply invaded schooling, and we constantly hear educational theorists and administrators use it to define teaching competence. What are we to make of this kind of language to describe teaching?

In it I have spotted a profound contradiction. On the one hand this language, used so that teachers will be encouraged to make sense of their pedagogic lives, is thoroughly imbued with hope. Yet it is almost exclusively a language of *doing* for the future, not of *being* now. It permits no description of our "being" with children as being present with hope. The language of objectives, aims, teacher expectations, intended learning outcomes, goals, ends in view is a disembodied language of hope from which hope itself has been systematically purged. It is the language of hopeless hope. It is an impatient language that does not truly awaken. It is a language that so chops up hope into small bits that neither the king's horses nor the king's men will ever put it together again.

"Having measurable objectives" differs from "having hope." Expectations and anticipations easily degenerate into desires, wants, certainties, predictions. Thus teachers close themselves off from possibilities that lie outside the direct or indirect vision of those expectations. To hope is to believe in possibilities. Hope strengthens and builds.

The point is not that the curricular language of educational aims, objectives or instructional intentions is wrong. Seen in proper perspective, this language is probably a useful administrative convenience. Teachers have always planned what should take place in a particular course, class or lesson. The problem is that the "administrative" and "technological" have so penetrated the very lifeblood of our existence that parents and teachers are in danger of forgetting a certain other type of understanding: what it means to hope for and bear children, and then to take care of and hope for them. Recalling what thus seems to be forgotten belongs to being a parent or a teacher.

Not to do so has dire consequences. Teacher burnout, for instance. It is a modern example of nihilism. Higher values are losing heart. There is no answer to the question, "What's the use?" Actually, the nihilistic "What's the use?" is less a question than a sigh, a shrugging off of any suggestion that there might be cause for hope. Teacher burnout is not necessarily a symptom of excessive effort, of being overworked. It is the condition of not knowing why we are doing what we are doing. Burnout is the evidence of hopelessness, of no longer being able to find a positive answer to the sigh, "What's the use?"

"I wish I could be young again but know what I know now." Many of us are nostalgic about our childhood, and not because we want to be children again. What we really want to do is be able to experience the world the way a child does. We long to recapture a sense of possibility and openness — a confidence that almost anything is possible.

A young child knows that he or she cannot really perform superhuman feats, yet in play the child experiences that possibility. All kinds of things are possible when one is young, and the reward for both parents and teachers is the presence of hope. That is what a child can teach us. It is what a child *must* teach us if we are to be true and good parents and teachers.

The way we understand our children is a telltale of the way we understand ourselves. We truly open ourselves to a child's way of being when we are able to experience openness ourselves. The child needs that openness to make something of himself or herself. As parents and teachers we need that openness to be what we are and to examine what we have made of ourselves. We must openly examine ourselves in front of children, for we must model asking ourselves how life is to be lived so that children, used to the question, will freely ask it of themselves. To live responsibly as an adult is to always remain open to the question of how life is to be lived. Thus my living becomes a constant example for the child. Whether I like it or not, my life will be saying, "This is the way one must live." My responsibility toward a child constantly confronts me with the need to act. It constantly makes me express and conduct myself in such a manner that the child is asked to recognize in me and through me the image of mature adulthood.

That's the way we must learn from our children. We must be even better learners than they are, because they in turn must learn from us.

Atmosphere is a way of knowing

Father is working behind the typewriter. He is somewhat preoccupied and tense about the business at hand and the approaching deadline. Mark fiddles around in the corner of the study and bumps his head. It is quite obvious he is not really hurt. Nevertheless he comes crying to his father. Mark's dad is a loving person, so almost automatically he pushes back his chair and takes Mark on his knee. "Oh boy, that was some bump. Let me give you a hug. Does it feel better now?" But these are only borrowed moments. Father cannot help feeling disturbed and interrupted in his work and concentration. It is noticeable in his voice and gestures. So Mark receives two messages. One says, "Come here and I'll attend to you." The other says, "Please leave me alone. I'm very busy." Then the interlude is over. "Why don't you go to Mama and show her where you bumped your head?" Mark complies, experiencing an atmosphere of ambivalence.

A trivial everyday occurrence. Life is full of contradictions and ambivalences. Why should we be surprised to discover that children experience uncertainties and insecurities?

Mother says, "I wonder if we should go for a skate or a swim." But her voice is flat and her gestures lack energy. So the children react with lukewarm enthusiasm, or maybe with indifference. What should spell fun and excitement is already cobwebbed with fatigue. The children have received ambivalent messages.

Every home, every classroom, every school contains a certain atmosphere. The question is not whether there should be a pervasive atmosphere in the school, but rather what kind is proper for it, worthy of it. "Atmosphere," as the word suggests, is a vaporlike sphere which envelopes and affects everything. The atmosphere in a church will hold a transcendent quality. A cabaret or bar may exude erotic sensuality. Tall modern architectures induce feelings of "modernity." Even entire cities hold specific pervasive moods, noted especially by travelers.

Homes and places of work have "atmosphere." Even small objects in them help to create special feelings and moods. This chair belonged to grandpa, and under that lamp grandma used to do her crafts. Both lamp and chair hold the warmth and love of parents for their children and grandchildren. The sense of mood or atmosphere is a profound part of our existence. By it we know the character of the world around us. Mood is a way of knowing and being in the world.

Schools too have atmosphere. Parents feel something of a school's mood during a parent-teacher interview. For a young child the school can have the feel of an alien and threatening place, or it can create an atmosphere which shelters the child and inspires him or her with security and confidence.

But the pervasive mood of a place, its atmosphere, is a complex phenomenon. A place which is experienced as threatening and intimidating by one child holds adventure and challenge to another. The mood of a place also depends on the disposition or frame of mind we bring to it. And yet it is true as well that the mood of a landscape, for example, or the beauty of evening light, can bring to us a stillness and sense of peace we did not know before. Atmosphere belongs to all aspects of human existence: to things (a spiritual painting, a cozy chair), to space (a peaceful landscape, a happy beach), to events (a festive graduation, a solemn speech), to time (a happy harvest, a thankful ending). Or better still, for each specific object or quality, atmosphere or mood is the way human beings experience the world.

Therefore, the recognition of the concept of atmosphere is pedagogically a positive phenomenon. Parents and teachers should understand the power of atmosphere to contribute to the general sense of being, and to the positive well-being of the child. A sensitive teacher is able to create or foster an atmosphere that is productive for certain kinds of living and learning. Teachers may not all agree on what specific qualities a school should hold, but no teacher will deny that school is a special place, and that therefore children should experience its corporeal, temporal and spatial dimensions in a manner good for them, pedagogically speaking.

Most teachers intuitively know this and therefore "dress up" the walls of classrooms with colorful displays and interesting materials. Yet even so, walls plastered with pictures, announcements of obligatory Christmas concerts, or other brightly colored materials may only create an atmosphere of inauthenticity, of mere busyness or shallow commitment. Some teachers seem to need to impress their colleagues and parents more than they need to edify the minds of the children who sit in their rooms all day.

So a teacher has to learn to become sensitive to the ways children experience the complexity of elements that contribute to the atmosphere of the school and classroom. The school is special in the same sense that the home is special: it is a place where we provide children with time and space to explore the world without becoming part of it. On the one hand, school is a protective enclave, a shield against various realities for which children are not ready yet. On the other hand, it is a place where the private and personal space of home is expanded to take in larger public or community space. In this sense the school mediates between home and the larger world.

As we walk into a classroom we like to feel that the atmosphere, even the sheer physical space, is sensitive to the need for intimacy, security and shelter as well as to the enticing call of a big world of public life and mysterious impersonal forces. When we enter a classroom, we soon have a sense of what pedagogy is practiced there. The atmosphere tells what vision the teacher has about what is a good space for children.

The lived space of the classroom, its textural and spiritual qualities, first should remind us of what schools are for. School is a place where children explore aspects of the human world. An elementary classroom speaks of the ways children come to know their world: mathematically, socially, historically, musically, literarily, aesthetically, and so forth. Rooms in secondary schools take on an atmosphere suited to individual subjects. A biology room is different from an art room, for example.

When a student enters an art class, her orientation shifts radically from the biology room she has just left. There the teacher discussed the structure and function of the human hand. She observed evolutionary characteristics in the hand bones of a primate, an Australopithecus and a modern man. She noted how the straightening of the fingers became more pronounced over time, and how the last phalanx of the thumb broadened and lenghtened. How useful an opposable thumb and its related musculature!

However, when she walks into the art appreciation class she notices a marvelous replica of Rodin's sculpture of the Praying Hands on the teacher's desk. Some students chuckle when they see it, as if caught by surprise. Sensitive fingers, extended upwards in a devoted plea, transcend their instrumental function. How miraculously expressed is their earth-bound spirituality. How different is the atmosphere in this classroom.

Two different realities, each with their own values, feelings, beliefs. How inappropriate it would be to attach terms like *saddle joint, abductor pollicis* and *the evolution of the last phalanx of the pollex* to Rodin's hands. How can one familiar hand be part of two such different realities?

As I write this I look at my hands over the typewriter keys. Such strange objects. I am taken back to a poem by Rainer Maria Rilke. He recalled once how, in reaching under the table, he saw his own hand groping, and for a moment it seemed that this "thing" had a life of its own. It seemed a foreign object, something in a different world acting on its own mysterious impulses. I recall the images of this sensitive poet, for they left an indelible impression on my mind. I try to remember the exact words, but my eyes glance at the preceding paragraph and instantly I am back in my classrooms and marvel once more at the shifts of mood that come when hands are set in different atmospheres.

Carefully we create an atmosphere in our home when we choose the color on the wall, the nature and arrangement of the furnishings, the placing of all the little things we grow so accustomed to that we get to see them only when they are missing. So teachers carefully, sensitively arrange their classrooms.

Some displays speak to children about the tasks school demands. They bring to mind that life requires a certain order. There is a time for everything. School is a place where one learns to mediate between lived time and clock time, leisure time and time on task, time for scheduling and completing things, personal time and collective time, beginning time and the sigh of ending.

Other aspects of the classroom bring to the child lived aspects of the world which home and neighborhood may lack. An urban classroom should remind children that all is not concrete and plastic. There are organic materials as well: wool, cloth, earth, clay, and plants. In this way the school balances the otherwise impoverished world of the child.

Displays and furnishing in the classroom may also serve to reinterpret the significance of past learnings. First Lucy studies spiders in class. Then she finds a little spider at home in the corner of her bedroom. She discusses with her father what she should do with the little creature. Capture and release it outside her window? Leave it there? Better leave it. The next day it has settled near the light fixture on the ceiling. Better leave the window ajar just a bit, enough to provide the spider with the option of staying or going. In school Lucy now scrutinizes once again the pictures and drawings of spiders on display, for the little leggy friend at home has taught her to look at the pictures with renewed interest. Old questions acquire new meanings, and new questions emerge. "What does a spider see?" "Would he see me?" "Is he a he or a she?"

Atmosphere is the way in which space is lived and experienced. But atmosphere is also the way a teacher is present to children, and the way children are present to themselves and to the teacher. Mood is set by bodily gesture and tone of voice. When the teacher reads Oscar Wilde's story *The Happy Prince,* a mood of spiritual beauty and sensitivity interweaves with the mood of storytelling itself. The teacher's voice breaks a little toward the end, and it deepens the catharsis for quite a few of the children. How can love sacrifice itself so beautifully, and yet so sadly for the little swallow?

When the teacher slowly closes the book, there is silence in the room. Even those children who were not really touched by the story refrain from talking for a moment. This silence has mood as well. It is not just an absence of sound or voices. It has a tonal quality all its own. In the stillness of the book that closes, the story lingers and charges the silence with reflection. It is the silence of reflection, of reckoning. This silence has a different atmosphere from the silence that reigns when every child is working individually at a math text.

The experience of curiosity and wonder

"What is that?" When a one-year-old begins to question the world, adults too easily misinterpret the "What is that?" question. "What is that?" asks Jeff as he points at a car going by. The parent might answer, "But Jeff, you know what that is. It's a car, of course." *Car, truck,* and *bus* were among the first words Jeff learned. But it is very normal for little children to direct their "What is that?" questions to the familiar objects of their everyday experience.

"What is that?" does not ask for a simple answer. The young child who asks it is looking for more — for an adult to converse about the world. "What is that?" asks for time to dialogue, time to think, to wonder, to marvel. So rather than simply naming the objects the child points to, the adult might dwell on the different meaning dimensions of that object. Indeed, naming something is more than learning to label it. Naming something is getting to know what that thing really *is*, what it is in its *whatness* and *thatness*.

Children are naturally curious about almost everything. The adults in a child's life need to understand the nature of that child's curiosity. What should we do with a child's questions? Schools are often blamed for extinguishing natural curiosity, for quelling the interest children have in learning why things are the way they are and how they come about. But is curiosity a good thing? What kind of curiosity should be encouraged?

Ben has a keen interest in insects, and for a five-year-old he knows a good deal about them. Often he and his father go to a creek or a woods to collect some. Later they look at them through a microscope. Ben's father is a scientist, and soon Ben is known among his friends as a person who knows a lot about science. "If you want to know about insects, then ask Ben."

Christopher is also interested in insects, and he is a close friend of Ben. But sometimes Chris is quite upset about Ben's behavior. Just the other day they discovered a caterpillar in the backyard and Ben stepped on it, killed it. Then yesterday afternoon Chris and Ben were playing outside when they noticed a big lazy spider. Ben rushed into the house for a glue bottle and dripped glue on the creature. Later he put glue on a beetle and some ants. That night Christopher had dreams about spiders and beetles who cried for help, and ants who were dying in large numbers.

It is obvious that Ben and Chris "know" insects in a different way. What is remarkable is that, from a pedagogic point of view, these differences are consolidated from a very early age. For Ben, the spider, the beetle, the caterpillar, the ants are merely creatures to be collected and classified. They are interesting, to be sure, but Ben lacks a sense of *deep* interest in them. He knows how many legs there are on a spider, what a beetle's body is made of, how caterpillars metamorphose, and how strong ants are for their size. But while for Ben the world of little creatures is full of mysterious phenomena, for Christopher it is full of facts. The difference is that Ben is unlearning something that comes naturally with childhood: the ability to wonder, and to feel awe and reverence for the ways of nature.

Children who are curious are always asking questions. Impossible questions. Which animal is the biggest? Which one is the fastest? What happens when you pull a spider's leg? How many stars are there in the sky? How can Superman be so strong? However, the impossibly curious child is not the one who wonders too much, but the one who wonders too little. There is a kind of precocious curiosity that is merely incidental and shallow, and it will contribute little to a child's proper growth.

Questions are impossibly curious (precocious) when they hurry the child too hastily into a premature grasping of phenomena for which a child is simply not ready. A precocious child has learned too many answers to questions which for the time should remain open and indeterminate. A precocious child knows a great deal, or at least *seems* to. But really, he or she knows only many answers to many questions, most of which were never real questions to begin with. Most of the questions by precocious children are fleeting questions. They do not emerge out of real preoccupations, out of genuine interest. Rather, curiosity merely leapfrogs around. What is of interest this moment is discarded the next, replaced by new fleeting interests.

An impossibly curious child has already learned the wrong thing from adults: questions can be stopped by answers. This kind of child experiences questioning as a kind of game, a game of finding answers that stop questions dead in their tracks. There is a certain feeling of security in a world where, at least in principle, every question has an answer — in a world where we experience things as being solidly grounded, where every question finds its place in some rock-bottom sense of natural order and certainty. And yet this security is a false one.

Rather than seeing a child's question as something that needs a quick and simple answer, the adult should try to help the child in his or her natural inclination to *live* the question. I wonder why the sun is so hot? I wonder how the earth was made? I wonder where I came from? I wonder why the leaves turn color and fall off trees? Each of these questions is worth pausing for. True wonderment does not ask a thousand questions. I truly wonder when the question I ask is returned to me somehow, or when it lingers and envelopes itself with a stillness, the stillness of wonder.

An effective parent or teacher is not necessarily one who can answer the rapid fire of a child's questions. It might also be one who can catch a question and deepen it with a quiet gesture.

"I have quite a few conversations with Mark about questions that concern and preoccupy him," says his kindergarten teacher. "This morning he asked, 'Where does the earth come from?' So I told him that people have been wondering about that question for a long time, and I offered him some of the stories people have provided as possible answers to it. I wanted to keep the question open for him, not fix it with an answer."

What is a good story to answer a child's question? A good story does not automatically orient the child to the natural order of modern science. The child is not necessarily asking for causal explanations of natural phenomena. "Why do the leaves turn color?" Many answers are possible: "It's nature's way of saying that trees need a rest." "The autumn leaves make the world beautiful before the winter arrives." "See how nice it is to smell and walk through the fallen colored leaves." An appropriate answer for a particular child is a story that belongs to that child. A good story provides an answer that remembers the child's interest in questioning. A tactful educator will keep alive the interest that produced the child's question.

How do children experience our presence?

It is surprising how perceptive young people are about the inconsistencies between what we say or do and what we are. Just as a true lover cannot be fooled for long by a partner's pretending, so a child cannot be misled by a teacher's fake enthusiasm or false expertise. A teacher who does not know what he or she is talking about (whether aware of it or not) is soon unmasked as one who should not be taken too seriously. "Teacher so-and-so isn't real," young people say.

A young and insecure teacher who desperately tries to feign an air of self-confidence soon gives away his or her real state of being. Children will quickly sense it in an awkward gesture, a false pose, a look in the eyes. So much that happens between teachers and students transpires through the face and eyes. A powerful teacher is a man or woman who has a powerful presence. Let us explore what it means to be present as teacher to some child or adult. It is sometimes said that we know a person by his or her deeds. In my experience, it is easier to observe and describe what we do than what we are.

If a teacher competently adheres to a set of curriculum objectives, but in a deeper sense does not know where he or she is going, if a teacher discusses poems but is unable to poetize life, if a teacher talks about responsibility but does not live a responsible life, if a teacher constantly assigns grades but fails to make perfection the standard of his or her own striving, if a teacher works hard at being liked by his students but then forgets what teaching really is, if a teacher knows many jokes to amuse students but lacks a true sense of the joy of being, if a teacher shows an eloquent command of language but produces mostly empty chatter, if a teacher effectively individualizes the curriculum but fails to really know children, if a teacher gives evidence of knowing the world but does not take responsibility for it, if a teacher is able to cite important educational aims and goals but is unable to live a deep sense of hope for each child, if a teacher integrates his or her subject with others but lacks a vision of the whole, if a teacher asks students many questions but does not truly know how to be addressed by a question, if a teacher acts with authority but does not know what authorizes him or her pedagogically, if a teacher (one could almost go on forever) . . . then the observable teacher behavior, what that teacher is doing overtly, is a profound contradiction of the way he or she exists in the world, or better, in the school, in this classroom, with these young people. Or maybe we should say that when a teacher fails to *be* what ostensibly he or she *does*, then that teacher is really an absence, is not at all genuinely present to those kids.

We may be physically present to children while something essential is absent in our presence. Similarly, we may be physically absent from children while in a different sense they remain present in our lives after school, and we remain present to them. This happens to a child doing homework who feels the teacher looking over his or her shoulder. Or to a teacher preoccupied with something that happened during the day who cannot put a particular child out of mind.

Whether we like it or not, adults cannot help being examples to children, either positive or negative examples. Children are experiencing adults as examples when they ask, "How come you always tell me to do this but you never do it yourself?" Or "Why do you care so much about my report card but you never take any interest in my work?" Or "Why do we have money for a new car but not for airplane tickets for visiting grandma?"

When an adult turns from merely being an example of *behaviors* children imitate to being a *real* example, living the great values he or she tells children to uphold, then that adult assumes pedagogic significance in children's lives. The adult is no longer a mere teacher of skills, a shallow television hero, a popular sports figure, or an entertaining parent. He or she has become a pedagogue — a true educator. What a thoughtful parent or teacher does is offer the young person a vision of what kind of life is worth living and what image of adulthood is worth aiming for.

Indeed, this is the meaning of learning. In early English, to "learn" meant to teach or to let learn, as well as to learn. It would then be correct to say that someone could "learn" someone to learn something. In the Dutch language, "to learn" *(leren)* is still used interchangeably for teaching and learning. "Teacher" is *leraar;* "student" is *leerling.* Etymologically, to learn means to follow the traces, tracks or footprints of one who has gone before. In this sense, the teacher or parent who is able to "let learn" therefore must be an even better learner than the child who is being "let learn."

We cannot be all things to all children. So when I call myself a math teacher, or a teacher of literature or history or science, I declare that I have available a vocational range of pedagogic possibilities and responsibilities. But what is it like to teach children literature or history? To be a teacher of history or literature may mean that I can tell many stories, or talk endlessly about poetry and the works of great poets. Obviously, to know a particular subject means that I know something in that domain of human knowledge. But to know something does not mean to know just anything about something. To know something is to know what that something is in the way it speaks to us, in the way it relates to us and we to it.

To know a subject does not only mean to know it well and to know it seriously in the fundamental questions it poses. To know a subject also means to hold this knowledge in a way which shows that it is loved and respected for what it is and the way it lets itself be known. We learn *about* the subjects contained in a school curriculum. It is also true that the subjects *let* us learn something about them. It is in this letting us know that subject matter becomes a true subject: a subject which makes relationships possible. Our responsiveness, our "listening" to the subject, constitutes the very essence of the relationship between student and subject matter.

Water (H_2O) is its chemical and physical properties, of course. But it is also the cooling (or uncomfortable) rain on our body, the habitat of fish and fowl, a necessity for the growth of our food, an opportunity for profit, a reason for war, a cascade of beauty, a confirmation of religious grace.

Some people think it does not matter whether teachers know a great deal about the subjects they teach. Good teaching is determined by the how (teaching method or style) rather than the what (content), or so the thinking goes. So we often see high school physical education teachers in front of English classes, or physics teachers teaching history. However, there is deep truth in the statement "you are what you teach." A math teacher is not (or should not be) just somebody who happens to teach math. A real math teacher is a person who *embodies* math, who *lives* math, who in a strong sense *is* math. We can often tell whether a teacher is "real" or "fake" by the way that person stylizes what he or she teaches. Indeed, a fake is incapable of stylizing what he or she does not embody in the first place. When a person says, "That's not my style," the statement means, "That's not the way I am. That's not me."

The way we stylize subject matter is a telltale expression of the way we hold it. We may possess a certain amount of information in literature, math, or science, but only the knowledge we embody has truly become part of our being. A real English teacher tends not only to love reading, writing, and carrying poetry under one arm during coffee break; a real English teacher cannot help but poetize the world — that is, think deeply about human experience through the incantative power of words.

There is much to be learned from what students say about outstanding teachers they have had. Or from hearing them describe the teachers they learned best from, the ones they would like to be themselves. Certain themes will begin to emerge, themes hidden behind stories and anecdotes that easily lead to generalizations about such teachers being fair, patient, able to communicate, keeping good discipline, having a sense of humor, being interested in and knowing children, knowing what to teach.

But the themes behind these generalizations are harder to put into words. At an even deeper level, teacher competency has more to do with pedagogical tactfulness, having a sensitivity to what is best for each child, having a sense of each child's life and his or her deep preoccupations. It also includes a sense of the aspects that draw the curriculums of math, English, social studies, art, or science to the curriculum of life itself.

When a child tells real-life stories of how he wanted to be trusted and believed by a teacher, he or she also touches on that deeper sense of trust and belief without which a teacher is no longer an educator. When students say that teachers should like what they teach and have a sense of humor, but that they should "not always try to be funny or tell dumb jokes," then they point in the direction of what it really means to be what you say or do as a teacher: to have a sense of joy and deep commitment to life, to the world, and to the subject matter that draws teacher and students into the world. When students say that teachers should "know what students need," "help them with homework," "be available to them," and "not hand out work and then walk out the door," that teachers should "have patience" and "not give up on kids," then they have pointed once again to the essence of pedagogic competence: a teacher who gives up on a child, who no longer knows how to have a sense of hope for that child, immediately steps back from being a teacher. When students say "good teachers know how to make you learn," "good teachers know how to make you like math or science or English even though you always hated it," "good teachers are enthusiastic about what they teach," then they refer to another essential aspect of teaching: a good teacher does not just happen to teach math or poetry; a good teacher embodies math or poetry. Good teachers *are* what they teach.

Competence is a way of being with children

Every adult responsible for a child needs to cultivate thoughtfulness and tact. But tact is a competence that few books in education (if any) talk about. Why not? I think because it cannot be described in a direct and straightforward manner. However, we can describe pedagogic tact indirectly, by way of examples and anecdotes. This is what I have attempted to do. I have described it as a particular sensitivity and attunement to situations. No theoretical knowledge, no rules or general principles of how to behave tactfully can be found. And yet it is possible for parents and teachers to cultivate both thoughtfulness and tact.

How can we do it? First we need to understand the physical nature of knowledge. How intimately the human body is connected to the human spirit! It is often said that the eyes are the mirror of the soul. That means that human beings mirror themselves from the inside, and the world mirrors itself from the outside. Through the senses we are connected as seeing, hearing, and touching beings with our children.

Think, for example, how we experience a glance. In a glance we see and are seen. In a glance the soul mirrors or expresses itself. And so we meet the soul of the other in a glance of love or hate, trust or fear, in a warm or cold glance, in an admiring or despising glance, in a glance of severity or leniency, confidence or unease, in a glance of caring or indifference, hope or despair, in an open glance or a deceiving one.

Through a glance we know the other and the other knows us. But, for a truly discerning knowledge of the soul of the other we need to refine our ability to see and interpret a glance. We need to know the importance of small things in our dealings with children. The big things are always in the small! We need to know how a meaningful wink can be more consequential sometimes than a barrel full of words. A perceptive teacher realizes when to be silent, when a small gesture is appropriate, when to pass over something with an understanding smile. Silence speaks. Sometimes the finest moments with a child, as with any friend, are spent in the comfortable company of silence.

And then there is the glance of passion for knowledge. No fanaticism or faked enthusiasm, but a glance which betrays how knowledge is absorbed in the teacher's personal forms of thinking, feeling, and acting. The example of a glance is important for illustrating that methods or techniques of teaching cannot be adequately described by external knowledge.

Imagine that we have just observed a rowdy classroom. Here is a classic example of a beginning teacher who does not know how to effect discipline in a classroom, helplessly facing taunting students, defiant looks in their eyes. Now observe another teacher. One admonishing glance in response to a smart remark from a student is enough for this teacher to settle the same class down to work. How can one teacher be so ineffective while another has only to look at the class to establish authority? Could one *learn* how to control a class with a glance? Could one write a ''how to'' book to help others learn? Not likely. To treat the glance as a mere teaching technique is to treat the knowledge of the glance as external. An effective teacher can be effective with a glance because the teacher *is* the glance. The glance is already the teacher's way of living and understanding the classroom situation.

Of course it is entirely possible that the glance of an ''effective'' teacher is effective only in silencing a class into intimidation, fear, or oppression. Such authority is not true pedagogic authority. Such discipline is not true pedagogic discipline. So we need to be aware how we, as teachers, are known by our children as we are captured in turn by their glance.

49

We may want to be encouraging to an unsympathetic child who needs encouragement. We may say the "right" words, but our glance betrays our true feelings. Through a glance we are immediately known to each other. A sobering realization. A glance cannot be manipulated in the same way as words can be shaped to suit our purposes.

And yet there is a practical implication in our understanding of the nature of a glance. On the one hand we can learn to sharpen our acuity of "seeing." On the other, we need to realize that we cannot easily (if at all) cover over our own glance. From minute to minute children and teachers are involved in reading from the face of the other what is disquieting, moving, boring, interesting, or disrupting. Children automatically check what we say with our mouths against what we say with our eyes. If the mouth and the eyes contradict each other, they are more likely to believe the eyes (the glance) than the mouth (the words).

And so, to cultivate pedagogic thoughtfulness and tact one needs to act in such a away that the glance expresses the soul's capacity for pedagogic relationship. In other words, pedagogic thoughtfulness and tact are not simply a set of external skills to be acquired in a workshop. A living knowledge of parenting or teaching is not just head stuff requiring intellectual work. It requires body work. True pedagogy requires an attentive attunement of one's whole being to the child's experience of the world.

Secondly, to cultivate our pedagogic thoughtfulness and tact we need to learn the significance of discipline. Discipline is not just the measure of order in our classroom. Discipline is the measure of our own orientation to order. Or rather, discipline is a way of talking about what matters to a person, how a person is oriented and stands in life. The roots of the word "discipline" refer to following, learning, and teaching. A disciple is one

50

who can follow a great teacher or a great example.
The word *docere* (to lecture) is also related to
discipline.

A disciplined person is prepared to learn and
to be influenced toward order. So the teacher needs
discipline as much as the student does. Without
discipline, a willingness to learn, there is no point
in the idea or existence of school. So to create
discipline in students, or in oneself, is to create
conditions for real learning. That is why it is often
said that true discipline in the classroom cannot be
separated from what is being taught or learned.
The deeper meaning of "discipline" has little to do
with the application of punishment, or with
authoritarian rule.

In a beautiful story called "The Star Thrower,"
the late Loren Eisely, professor of anthropology and
the history of science, recounts an experience that
marks this difference: Eisely is walking at an ocean
beach. There are people collecting shells and
starfish which the receding waters have strewn
along the shoreline. As he walks past the boiling
pots of the shell collectors and the starfish
gatherers, Eisely notices a lone figure in the far
distance. A man is gazing fixedly at something in
the sand. Eventually he stoops and flings an object
beyond the breaking surf.

When Eisely finally gets near, he sees the man
stoop again. In a pool of sand and silt a starfish has
thrust is arms up stiffly and is holding its body
away from the stifling mud. With a quick, yet
gentle movement the man picks it up and spins it
far out into the sea. "It may live," he says to Eisely.
Eisely is a bit embarrassed. He notices that no other
people have ventured so far down the beach. "Do
you collect?" he asks. And while gesturing at the
threatened life lying on the shore, the man says
softly, "Only like this. And only for the living."

What Eisely points out with this story is that
the essence of the discipline of science is not simply
collecting and classifying nature for the worldly

uses of humans. To be truly disciplined is to be a "thrower." The one who saves and restores. The one who labors to understand the nature of nature, for the sake of the natural, for the "uses of life." The star thrower he describes is possessed by a passion — the passion of a knowledge which is disciplined, which requires obedience and responsibility. Here "obedience" means being able to listen to what speaks or to what is being said. And to be able to hear stars, one must love their nature.

So far I have tried to show that in order to cultivate one's pedagogic thoughtfulness and tact one needs to understand the physical nature of pedagogic knowledge. And this requires discipline. Theories of teaching which concern mostly external forms of knowledge are of little consequence for our acting. A man who becomes a father learns to observe his children with father eyes, with a father body. Can anyone observe a child quite in the same ways a father does? And what is the nature of mother eyes? Can anyone else see the way a mother sees her child? A mother once said of her stepchild, "When I wipe his nose it's just a nose. But," she continued, "when I wipe my own son's nose I'm dealing with my child."

The practical consideration for a teacher is that he or she must believe that there is a pedagogic way of being with children that sets a teacher-child relationship apart from any other kind of adult-child connection. And a teacher who is disciplined is always asking what makes a certain situation or relation with a child pedagogic rather than something else.

Therefore, the third aspect of cultivating one's pedagogic thoughtfulness and tact is the need to act deferentially toward the difference that pedagogy makes. A teacher who is a true educator always offers his or her actions as a solution for what education is, for what it means to be inspired and guided by pedagogy.

For this reason, while a teacher may be there for the children, it is not primarily to be loved by or buddy-buddy with them. As a lover is guided by love, as a friend is guided by friendship, so a teacher is guided by pedagogy. Unfortunately it is only in real life that the concrete meaning of pedagogy is discernible. In a way, a lover's understanding of love is constantly tested in real life. So it is for teachers. The problem is that one usually does not know the test situation beforehand. Tests that are predictable no longer test.

New parents and beginning teachers tend to be amateurish in their thinking and acting. When confronted with a significant moment, they tend to think first, "What does the book say?" And when they then act, the significant moment is often gone. A professional, in contrast, takes the moment first, and then thinks about it. A professional can act first because his or her body has been readied by thoughtfulness. Or to say it differently, educators can act pedagogically at significant moments because they are already animated by the spirit of pedagogy.

A woman who finds herself pregnant is a changed woman. She is not changed only locally in her womb; her whole body, her very being is changed. Before, she might have had little interest in children, but now she sees children all around her. Some women say that to their surprise they feel, for the first time, the urge to hold a child, or to help a child in need. In a sense a mother-to-be is exercising herself, exercising her body, and being exercised by her body for motherhood.

Just so with teachers. Teachers who are "pregnant" exercise their bodies for teaching. A teacher who reads a significant book about children tends to read with teacher eyes. In this way teachers gain thoughtful knowledge of pedagogy, which makes tactful acting possible at significant moments.

53

Children are natural forgivers

When my wife, who is both a mother and a school teacher, read the manuscript for this book she said, "It speaks to me, but it makes me feel guilty." It is true. While writing this text I also constantly felt a personal sense of falling short of what a "true father," a "real teacher" should be. So what should we do with such feelings?

First, I do not believe in self-flagellation, which is self-indulgence. Moreover, both parents and teachers are too busy to surrender to feelings of remorse over past failings. We must get on with life, do the best we can.

On the other hand, I do not want to disregard my past and ongoing failures either. Realizing how I did the wrong thing for a child constantly gives me a measure of the true meaning of pedagogy. I let the term "reflective dialectic of pedagogic praxis," derived from my academic busyness, roll around in my head. "Reflective dialectic" refers to a constant alertness to the question of what education is, a constant measurement of my action against pedagogy. "Pedagogic praxis" refers to thoughtful action: action full of thought and thought full of action.

After all, as educators we must act ongoingly in our living with children. We may take some time out, personal time or simply time away from children. But even so, there really is no time off, short of running away from life itself. Once a parent always a parent. Once a pedagogue always a pedagogue.

So what should we do with the guilt of being an imperfect mother, father, teacher? We should do what I have urged throughout this book: look closely at our children. Children are natural forgivers, and that makes our responsibility to be true parents and teachers even more urgent. We must not abuse their forgiveness.

54

Children forgive their parents simply by loving them. The teacher, *in loco parentis,* uses the primordial parent-child relationship in which the child wants to please the parent as a resource for developing a pedagogic relationship. It would be difficult to overestimate the significance of a child's love for a parent. A child may have been hurt physically or emotionally, but the need to re-establish a loving relationship with the parent is always there. As children grow older there is often a time when they are more distant for a while, more inclined to judge the parent or teacher who hurts them. But usually these feelings get resolved, and then forgiveness is rooted in "understanding."

Contrary to a common saying, to forgive is not necessarily to forget. But forgiving has its own pedagogic value: restoring the relationship between parent and child, between teacher and student, through love and understanding.